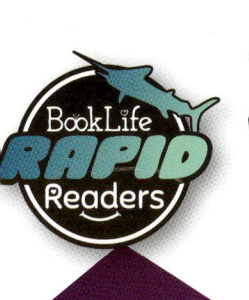

TOTALLY EXTREME FACTS

CAR FACTS

All rights reserved.
Printed in India.

Written by:
E.C. Andrews

©2024
BookLife Publishing Ltd.
King's Lynn, Norfolk
PE30 4LS, UK

A catalogue record for this book is available from the British Library.

Edited by:
Noah Leatherland

ISBN: 978-1-80505-688-1

Designed by:
Jasmine Pointer

All facts, statistics, web addresses and URLs in this book were verified as valid and accurate at time of writing. No responsibility for any changes to external websites or references can be accepted by either the author or publisher.

AN INTRODUCTION TO BOOKLIFE RAPID READERS...

Packed full of gripping topics and twisted tales, BookLife Rapid Readers are perfect for older children looking to propel their reading up to top speed. With three levels based on our planet's fastest animals, children will be able to find the perfect point from which to accelerate their reading journey. From the spooky to the silly, these roaring reads will turn every child at every reading level into a prolific page-turner!

CHEETAH

The fastest animals on land, cheetahs will be taking their first strides as they race to top speed.

MARLIN

The fastest animals under water, marlins will be blasting through their journey.

FALCON

The fastest animals in the air, falcons will be flying at top speed as they tear through the skies.

PHOTO CREDITS Images are courtesy of Shutterstock.com. With thanks to Getty Images, Thinkstock Photo and iStockphoto. Cover – Adrien The, Olha Kostiuk, art-sonik, Victor Metelskiy, Alena Nv, hvostik, Pogorelova Olga, KingVector, Irina Adamovich. 4–5 – Mikbiz, Perfect_kebab, Brandon Woyshnis, Aleksandr Artt, SpicyTruffel. 6–7 – Daria Pushka, FernandoV. 8–9 – GEORGE STAMATIS, Pikovit, Claire, Slingerland, Nutkins.J. 10–11 – kateetc, I Pokotylo, johavel, Iurii Davydov, Karuna Tansuk, Alfmaler, VikiVector. 12–13 – lennystan, Nikita Anokhin, Polina MB, Gercen. 14–15 – Sopotnicki, WladD, GalinaBahlyk, Smarta, Svvell Design. 16–17 – asharkyu, Net Vector, betto rodrigues, 32 pixels. 18–19 – Blulz60, Boykov, HappyPictures, Double Brain, maryartist. 20–21 – Rodrigo Garrido, Ronn Hook, Fayzulin Serg, Avigator Fortuner, Denissenko Oleg. 22–23 – Mechanik, Maksim Shmeljov, Nigel Jarvis, Double Brain. 24–25 – Gestalt Imagery, Erica Finstad, vector arts and creative. 26–27 – VIAVAL TOURS, Mor65_Mauro Piccardi, Net Vector. 28–29 – Phonlamai Photo, Pavel Chagochkin, yokunen. 30–31 – PBabic.

CONTENTS

PAGE 4	Totally Extreme Cars
PAGE 6	The First Cars
PAGE 8	Wind-Up Cars
PAGE 10	Fancy Fuels
PAGE 12	Weird Wheels
PAGE 14	From Massive to Mini
PAGE 16	Printed Cars
PAGE 18	Craziest Car Races
PAGE 20	Super Stunts
PAGE 22	Mega Monster Trucks
PAGE 24	The Fabulous Hudson Hornet
PAGE 26	Amphibious Cars
PAGE 28	Flying Cars
PAGE 30	Super Crazy Cars
PAGE 31	Glossary
PAGE 32	Index

WORDS THAT LOOK LIKE THIS ARE EXPLAINED IN THE GLOSSARY ON PAGE 31.

TOTALLY EXTREME CARS

Cars are very helpful. A lot of children get to and from school in them. There is so much more to cars than just pressing down a pedal and going forwards.

Cars can be some seriously EXTREME machines.

There are so many kinds of cars. From flying cars to cars that run on wine and cheese, every car has its own quirk.

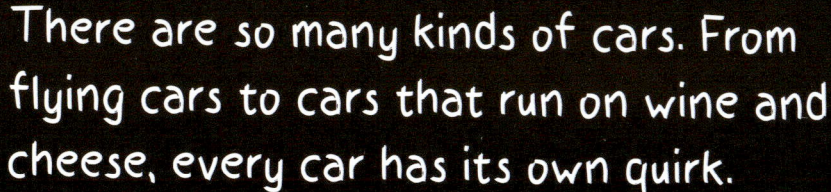

They are always different and always fascinating, sometimes in some seriously EXTREME ways!

THE FIRST CARS

Leonardo Da Vinci designed a car before anyone else in 1478. That was over 500 years ago! But Da Vinci never built it.

DA VINCI'S DESIGN

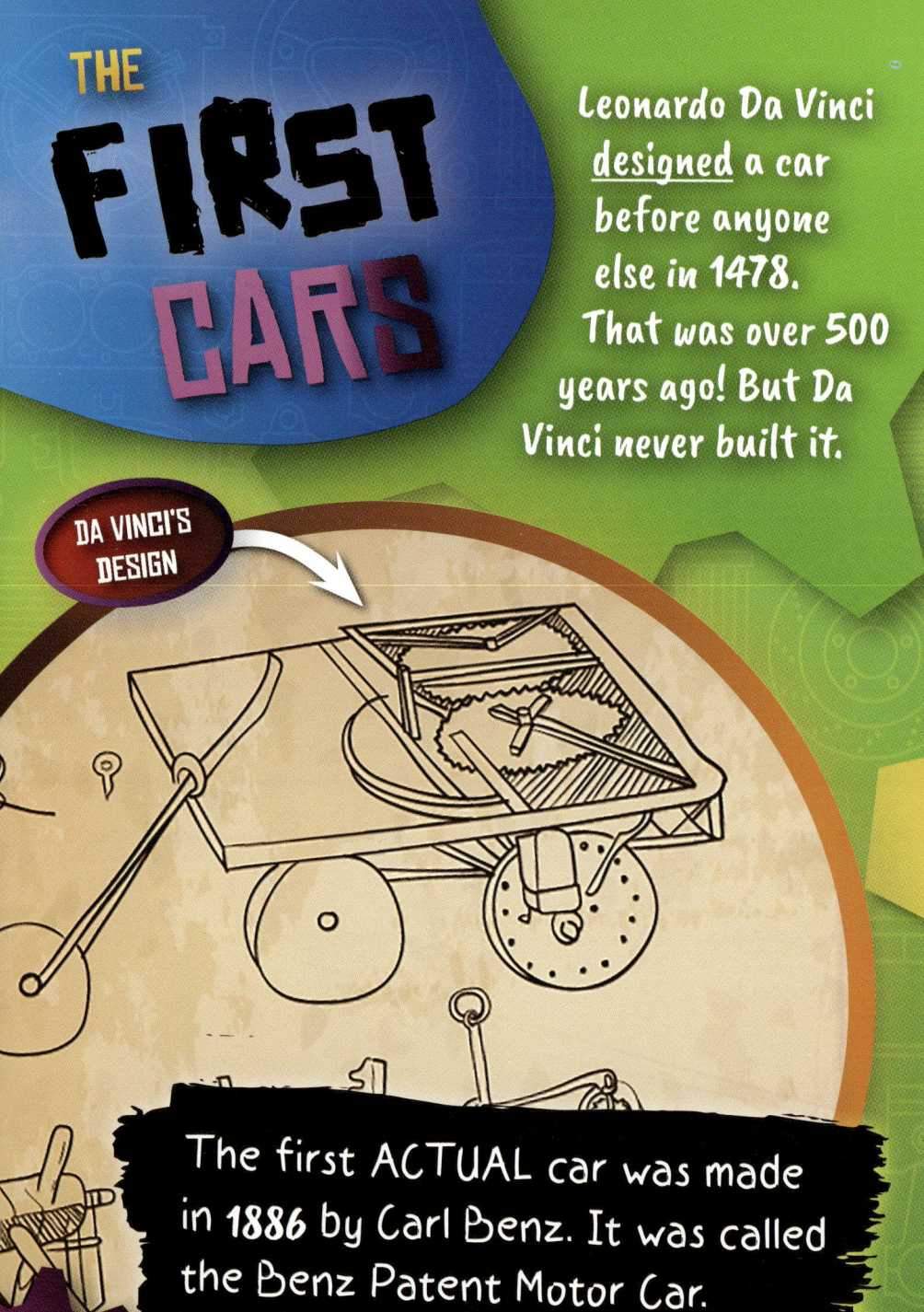

The first ACTUAL car was made in 1886 by Carl Benz. It was called the Benz Patent Motor Car.

The first long-distance journey in a car was made in **1888**. Carl Benz's wife, Bertha Benz, drove the car for **12** hours. But cars did not become popular until the **1920**s.

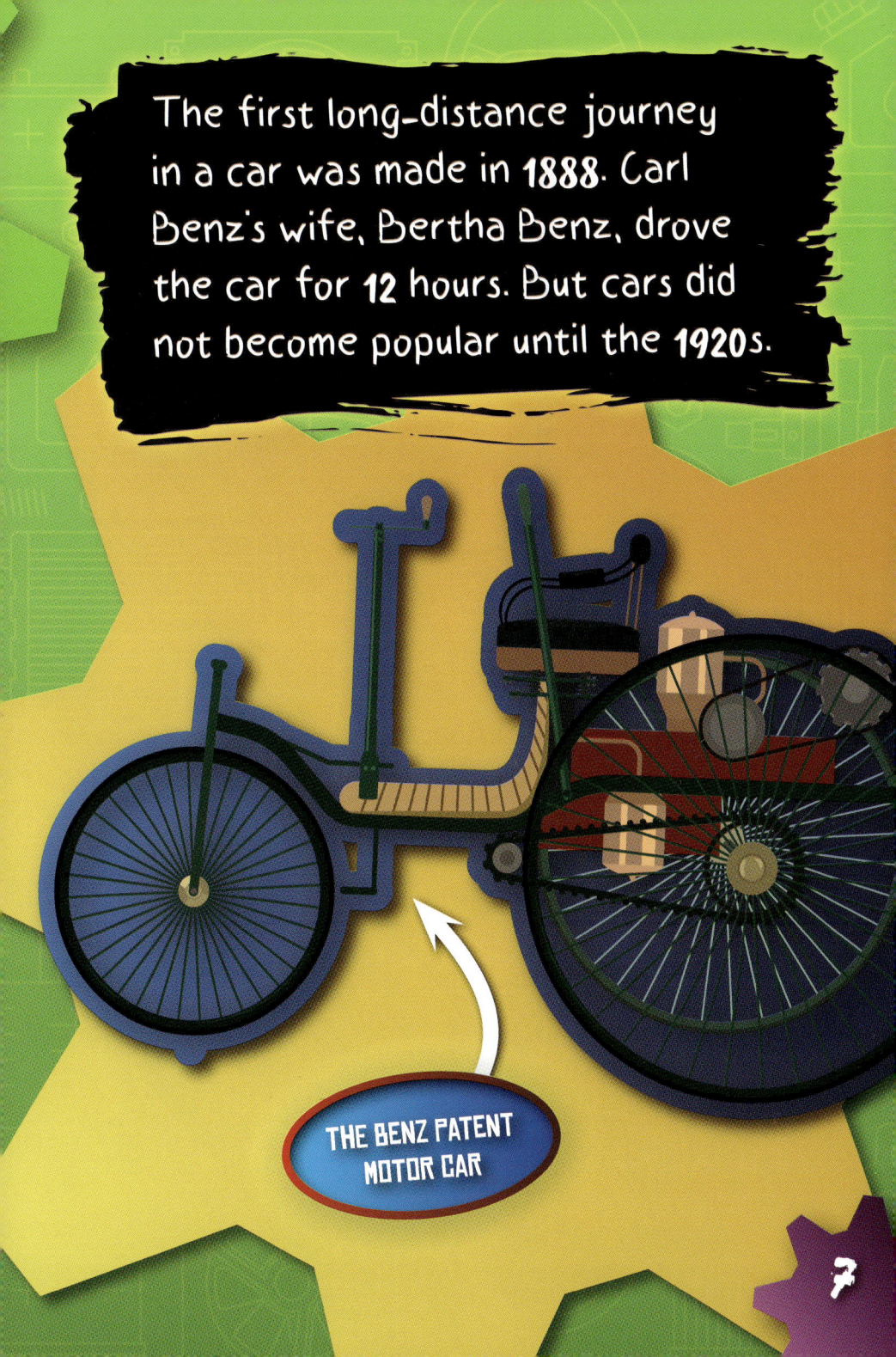

THE BENZ PATENT MOTOR CAR

WIND-UP CARS

The first cars were started using a wind-up handle called a crank handle. But you had to be careful.

SOMETIMES, THE HANDLE WOULD FLY OFF COMPLETELY AND HIT PEOPLE IN THE FACE!

Sometimes, the engine would start very suddenly and move the handle. Lots of people had their wrists broken by handles.

We do still use a tiny version of the crank handle on wind-up toy cars. The largest collection of wind-up toy cars belongs to a woman in California. She has **1,258** toy cars!

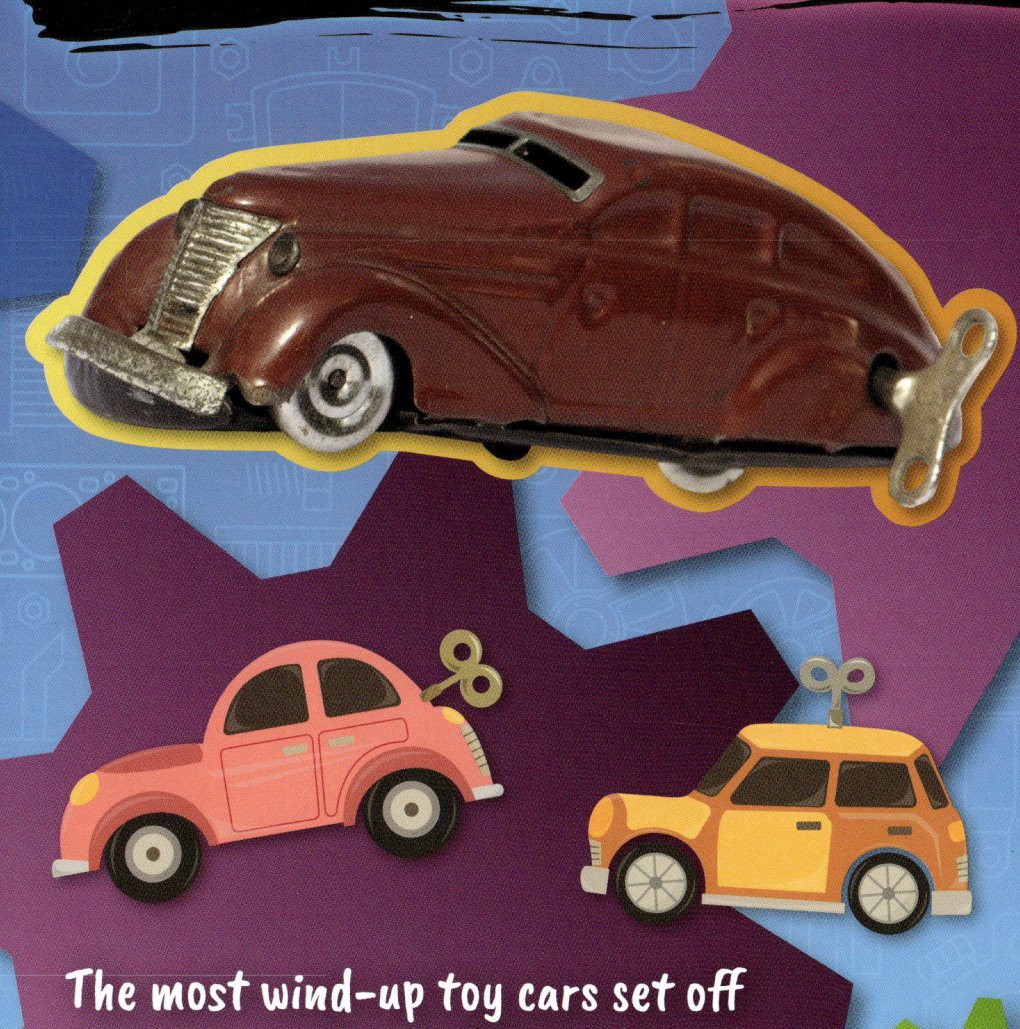

The most wind-up toy cars set off at the same time is 286.

FANCY FUELS

King Charles III of England owns a car that runs on white wine. It also uses whey as fuel. Whey is something that is left over from making cheese.

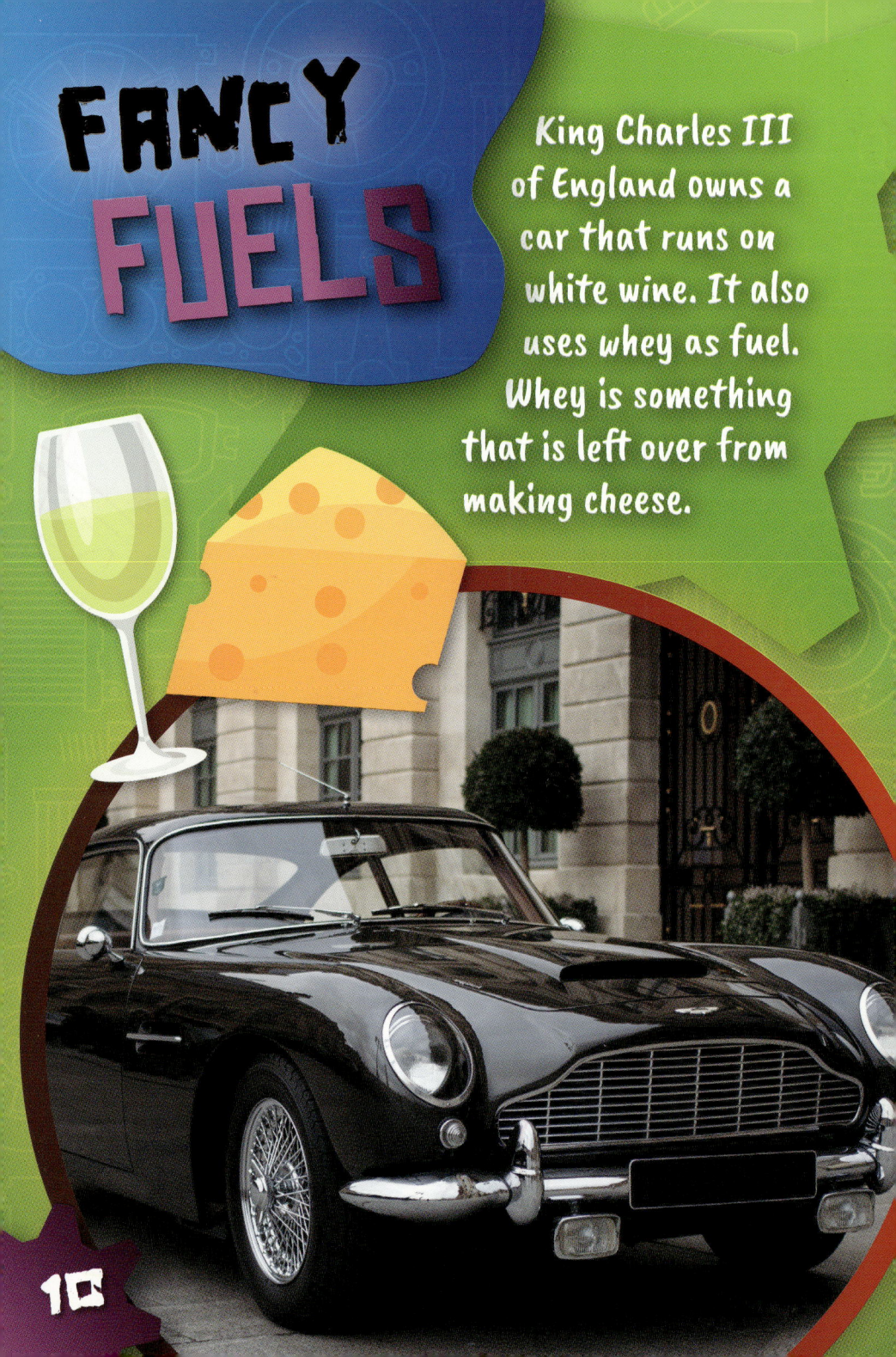

The King of England is not the only one. There are lots of cars that run on strange things. Some cars run on wood. Some run on coffee. Some cars even run on the fat left over from cooking French fries!

WEIRD WHEELS

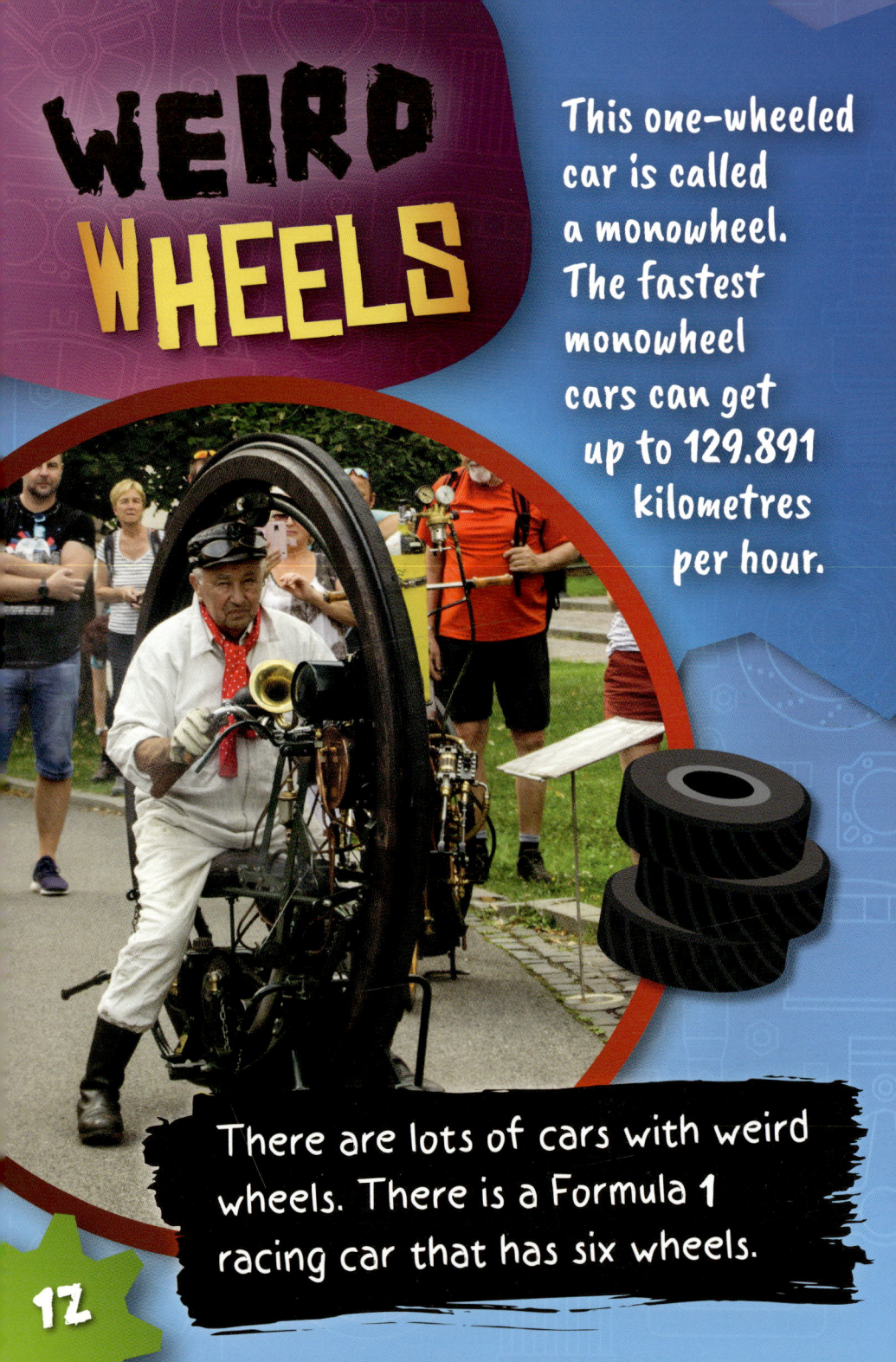

This one-wheeled car is called a monowheel. The fastest monowheel cars can get up to 129.891 kilometres per hour.

There are lots of cars with weird wheels. There is a Formula 1 racing car that has six wheels.

Some pick-up trucks have had tracks put over their wheels, just likes tanks. The three-wheeled High-Roller is shaped like a giant shoe.

There is a 26-wheeled car in the US that can fit up to 75 people! What else is packed inside?

FROM MASSIVE TO MINI

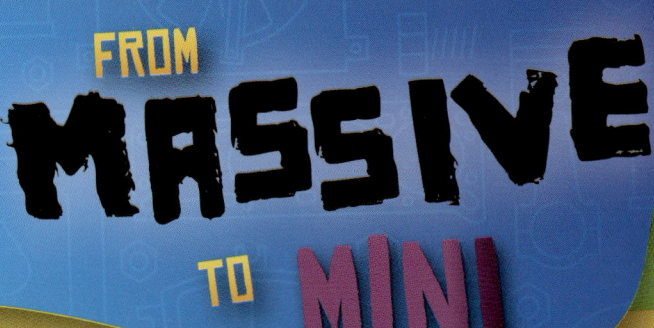

The American Dream is the longest stretch limousine in the world. It has 26 wheels.

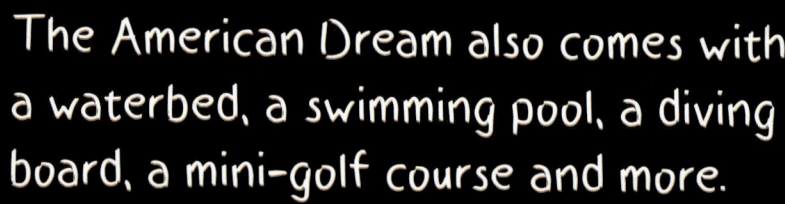

The American Dream also comes with a waterbed, a swimming pool, a diving board, a mini-golf course and more.

The American Dream may be massive, but some cars are absolutely mini! The Peel P50 is the smallest car ever made. It is 1.4 metres long. It only has three wheels.

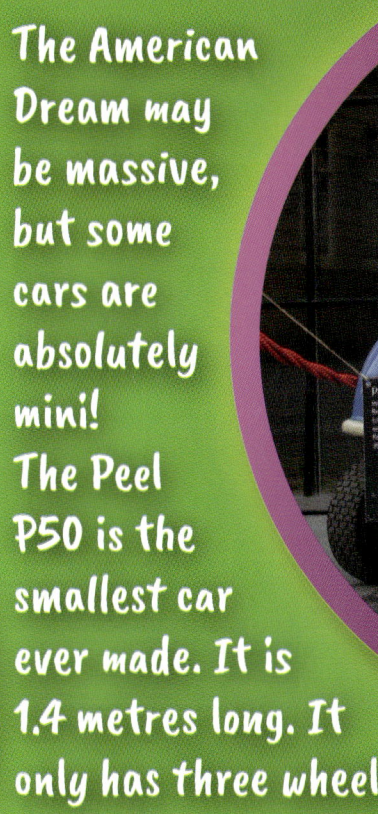

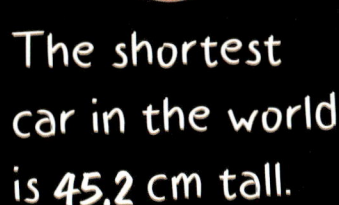

The shortest car in the world is 45.2 cm tall.

PRINTED CARS

3D printers can print whole cars. These printers have printed Formula 1 racing cars that can drive faster than 140 kilometres per hour.

A 3D PRINTER AT WORK

3D printers have even been able to rebuild rare cars from the olden days.

3D printers can also print modern cars. One of the coolest is this entirely 3D printed high-tech supercar.

It can go from 0 to 96 kilometres per hour in 2 seconds. It looks like it has time travelled here from the future!

CRAZIEST CAR RACES

Car races are EXTREME, but some are crazy and EXTREME.

SOAP BOX CAR

The Soap Box Derby is a race where the cars are made of actual boxes. Gravity pulls them downhill.

Racers in Florida like to challenge themselves by slamming heavy school buses around a racetrack. The racetracks of Norfolk in the UK race three-wheeled Reliant Robins.

Not all races are just about going fast. Endurance races have teams of drivers race for 24 hours straight!

Super Stunts

The fastest car wheelie was by a Finnish driver. He drove the car on two wheels at **185** kilometres per hour.

The longest jump in a car was done by an American driver. It was 101 metres long.

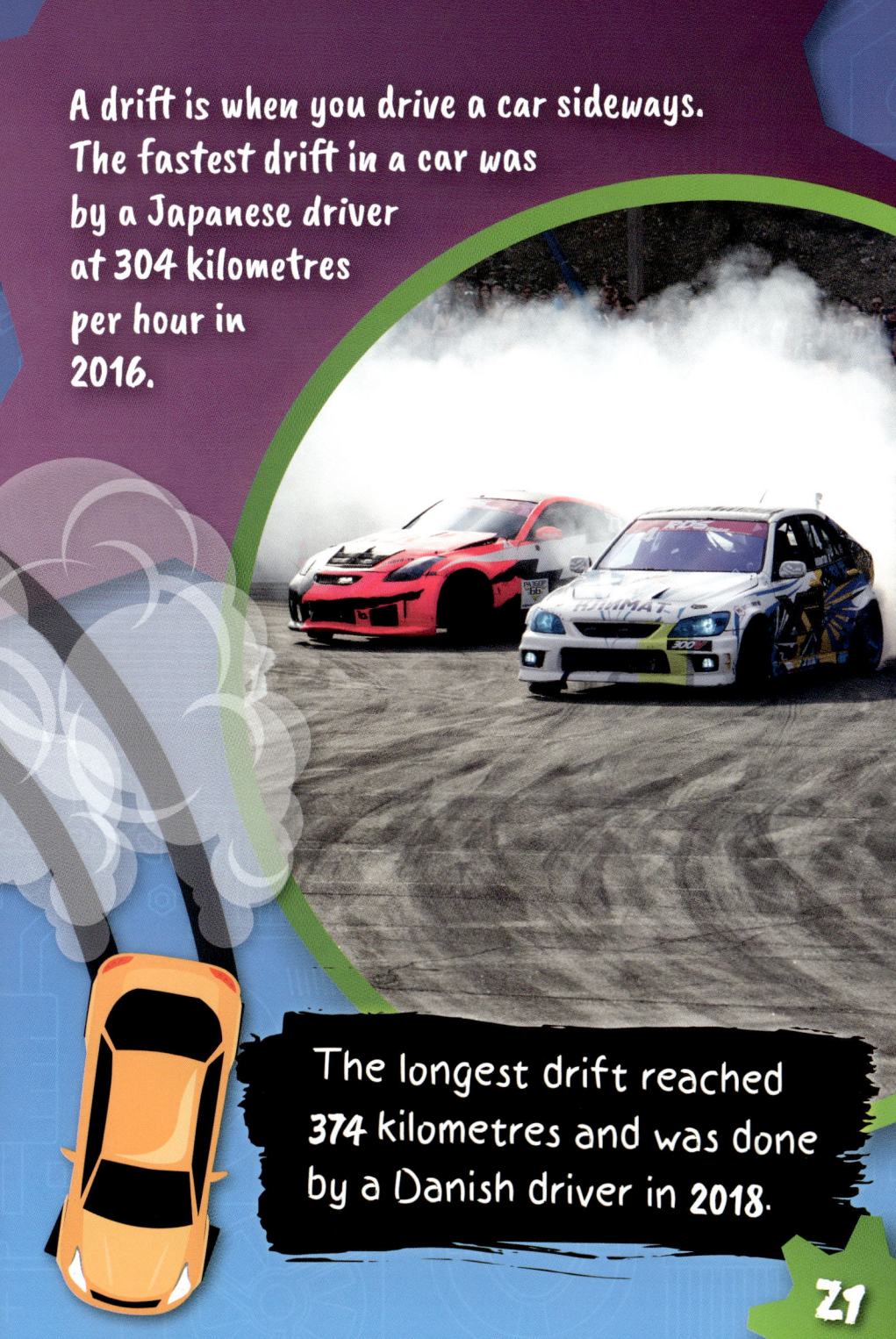

A drift is when you drive a car sideways. The fastest drift in a car was by a Japanese driver at 304 kilometres per hour in 2016.

The longest drift reached 374 kilometres and was done by a Danish driver in 2018.

21

MEGA MONSTER TRUCKS

The biggest monster truck in the world is called Bigfoot.

The Bigfoot truck is 4.7 metres tall. Bigfoot's tyres are three metres tall. Bigfoot also did the longest ramp jump in a monster truck at 72.42 metres.

The longest monster truck is called the Sin City Hustler. It is 9.75 metres long.

The record for the fastest monster truck goes to Bryce Kenny from Florida, who drove one of these heavy trucks at **162** kilometres per hour.

THE FABULOUS HUDSON HORNET

This is the Hudson Hornet. You might recognise it. But do you know its real story?

The Hudson Hornet was made in the early 1950s. At the time, it was one of the best race cars in America.

The Hudson Hornet won **79** races and three championships between **1951** and **1955**. In its prime, the Hudson Hornet was at the top of the American NASCAR races.

It won 27 out of 30 NASCAR races in 1952.

AMPHIBIOUS CARS

Some cars can drive across water as well as dry land. These are called <u>amphibious</u> cars.

The first <u>mass produced</u> amphibious car was built in Germany in **1961**. They became very popular in the US.

The first amphibious car to cross the English Channel was in **1958**. It took **7** hours and **33** minutes.

The fastest amphibious car to cross the English Channel was in 2008. It took 1 hour and 14 minutes.

FLYING CARS

Water cars are one thing, but what about flying cars? An aeroplane expert called Glenn Curtiss designed a flying car over 100 years ago in 1917. It was never fully tested. A fully electric flying car is now being designed in the US.

The Transition is a plane that can fold its wings away to become a road car!

A flying car is also being designed by a company in Slovakia. You might be able to buy one in the next few years.

29

SUPER CRAZY CARS

As you can see, there are some pretty EXTREME cars in the world. They all work in different ways, do different things and feel different to drive. They really are very fascinating machines.

GLOSSARY

AMPHIBIOUS	something that works on land and water
DESIGNED	planned for a specific purpose
EXTREME	at the highest level
GRAVITY	the invisible force that pulls everything downwards
MASS PRODUCED	things that are made in very large numbers
NASCAR	a type of car racing that is popular in the US
RARE	not being many of its kind and being hard to find

INDEX

DRIFTS 21

ENGINES 8

FORMULA 1 12, 16

FUEL 10

GRAVITY 18

LIMOUSINES 14

MONSTER TRUCKS 22–23

NASCAR 25

TOYS 9

WHEELS 12–15, 20